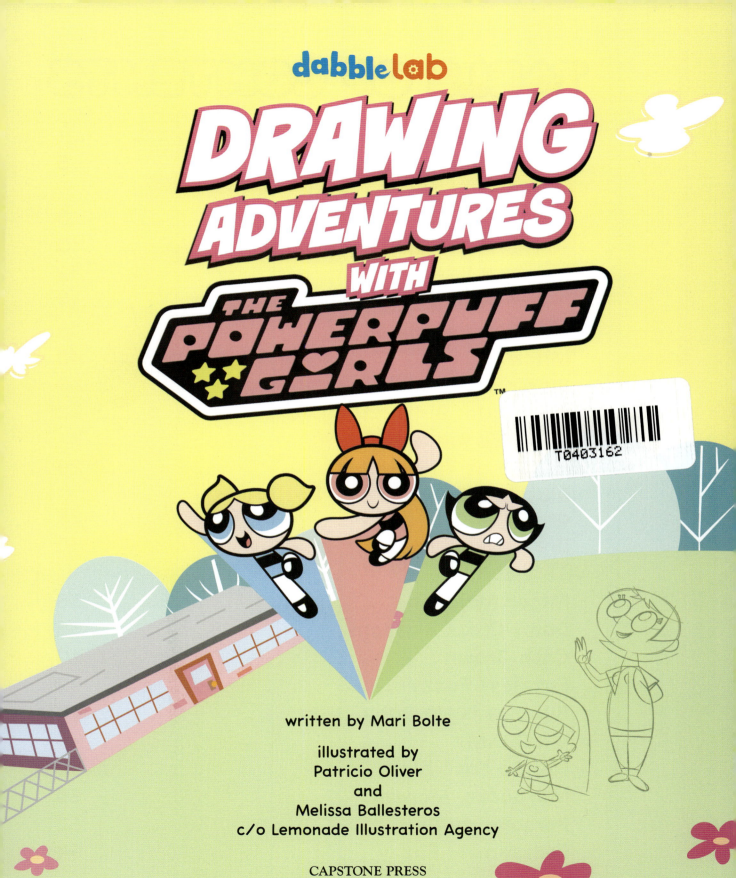

dabble lab
DRAWING ADVENTURES WITH THE POWERPUFF GIRLS

written by Mari Bolte

illustrated by
Patricio Oliver
and
Melissa Ballesteros
c/o Lemonade Illustration Agency

CAPSTONE PRESS
a capstone imprint

TABLE OF CONTENTS

Meet the Powerpuff Girls 4
The Cartoonist's Toolbox 5

FAVORITE FRIENDS

Powerpuff Girls to the Rescue! 8
Townsville's Number One Dad 10
Meet and Greet the Mayor 12
Keen on Keane 14
The Robin Next Door 16
Mitch Rocks. 18
Blossom's Ballad. 20
Batter Up, Buttercup! 22
The New Kid(s) in Town 24
Not What They Seem 26
Blossom, Bubbles, and Buttercup
at the Beach 28
Dream Scheme, Bedtime Routine 30

VILE VILLAINS

Major Mojo 36
Don't Cross Blossom! 38
Cash Crown 40
Fuzziest Fuzzy 42
Bubbles Is No Baby 44
V.R.O.O.M.! 46
Not So Fast, Mojo Jojo 48
Morbucks, Morevil 50
Personality Plus 52
Fearsomely Fuzzy 54

Get Rowdy 56
Good Girls vs. Bad Boys 58

MEAN MONSTERS
Beware: Bad Breath! 64
Game On, Monsters 66
Eye See You 68
Maggot Monster Madness 70
RSVP to the Birthday Bot 72
Cloudy with a Chance of Cheese 74
Meet the Gangreen Gang 76
Gangreen with Envy 78
Blowup Balloon 80
Here, Kitty, Kitty 82
The Monster Mash 84
Orange You Glad for Oranges? 86

PLAYFUL PETS
Warning: Chance of Falling BEEBO 92
Bubbles with Bubbles 94
Ruff Crowd 96
Nuts for Bullet 98
Pretty Witty Kitty 100
Plushie Power 102
Happy Valentino's Day 104
Big Baby 106
First of the Fluff 108
The Puppy Wuppy 110
Hop to the Scene of the Crime 112
The Powerpup Girls 114

About the Author 118
About the Illustrators 119

The perfect little girl doesn't exist—

Wait, wait, don't get mad! Let me finish! I was going to say: "The perfect little girl doesn't exist . . . because there are three of them!" Together, Blossom, Bubbles, and Buttercup fight crime and keep the citizens of Townsville safe.

That's no small feat, because every day brings something new. Whether it's making friends at school and around the city, battling scheming villains, facing down rampaging monsters, or snuggling with the cutest little pets, the superhero sisters stay busy.

So what are you waiting for? Grab your art supplies and go on an exciting drawing adventure!

THE CARTOONIST'S TOOLBOX

Anyone can put pen to paper and become a cartoonist. Just follow the steps, practice, and have fun! Here are a few tools and tips on how to bring the Powerpuff Girls and their friends and foes to life.

A **pencil** is one of the best drawing tools around! Keep it sharp. Lightly sketch characters first.

Have an **eraser** handy. You're bound to make mistakes, and that's okay! An eraser can also remove lines from earlier steps and polish up your drawing.

Grab a good fine-tip **black marker**. Trace your drawing when it's just how you like. Allow time for the ink to fully dry so it doesn't smudge.

Add a pop of color! **Colored pencils** and **markers** are great options. Bright colors help your finished drawing shine.

FAVORITE FRIENDS

POWERPUFF GIRLS TO THE RESCUE!

Once again, the day is saved thanks to the Powerpuff Girls! That's how most of the girls' adventures end. Why wouldn't they? Blossom, Bubbles, and Buttercup each have super speed and super strength. They can fly. They can see in the dark and blast out rays of heat vision. They can even survive in space! WOWZA! When these super sisters work together, there's nothing they can't do.

FACT

Blossom is the leader. She wears a showy bow. Bubbles is sweet. She has super-cute pigtails. Buttercup is tough. Her hair is short—just like her temper!

TOWNSVILLE'S NUMBER ONE DAD

Professor Utonium created a recipe for the perfect little girl. Sugar, spice, and everything nice! Sure, he also dropped some Chemical X in by accident. But it all worked out . . . because Blossom, Bubbles, and Buttercup were born! The Professor loves inventing. If he's not in the lab, he's in the kitchen. (Sadly, his food isn't as good as his science.)

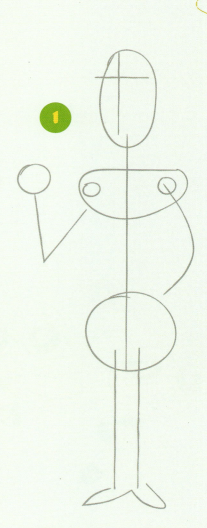

1

TIP
Pay attention to shapes as you draw characters. The Powerpuff Girls are mostly circles and curved lines. The Professor is more square with sharp edges.

MEET AND GREET THE MAYOR

Oh no! There's an emergency in Townsville! Luckily, the Mayor has a direct line to the most heroic heroes to ever hero. *Ring! Ring!* "Come quick, Powerpuff Girls!" As long as Bubbles doesn't hang up on him, help is (probably) on the way!

TIP
The Mayor likes accessories! Don't forget the buttons on his pointy shoes or the chain on his monocle. Little details make your art pop.

KEEN ON KEANE

Miss Keane is the best—and only—teacher at Pokey Oaks Kindergarten. Good thing she can handle the heat. What's her secret? Let's ask the class. Sorry, Bubbles, it's not a new cat. Fridays are now Food Fight Fridays? Nice try, Blossom. No, those aren't new pants, Buttercup. Stop asking. Maybe Miss Keane's secret is endless patience. Teachers are the real heroes.

FACT
The Powerpuff Girls once set Miss Keane up on a date with Professor Utonium. Sad to say, it didn't work out.

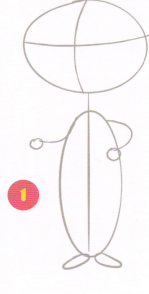

THE ROBIN NEXT DOOR

Friendship isn't always easy. Especially when your new BFFs are off saving the world! Robin Snyder wishes she could spend every afternoon hanging out with the Powerpuff Girls. But their fun keeps getting interrupted by bad guys. Will Blossom, Bubbles, and Buttercup learn to balance work with play? Or will Robin be left alone in the sandbox?

FACT
Robin likes dodgeball and drawing. She lives next door to the Powerpuff Girls.

1

16

MITCH ROCKS

Mitch Mitchelson is the bad boy of Pokey Oaks, and he's not going to let anyone forget it. Whether he's messing with the class pet, ruining Bubbles's art projects, or just being a pain, he likes causing a scene. But no matter how naughty Mitch may be, the rowdy boy is still Buttercup's best school friend.

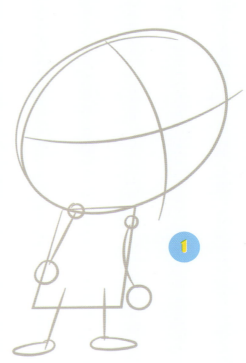

TIP
Write the words on Mitch's shirt in white pencil first. Then carefully add black around the letters, making sure to stay off the white.

BLOSSOM'S BALLAD

Hello? Sorry, Mr. Mayor, you'll have to call back later. Blossom is about to jam! She's got songs about feelings, fighting evil, and wishing for world peace. Now she's taking center stage. And with super speed, going on the road for a world tour is no problem either. Being a hero never sounded so good.

FACT
Blossom's guitar shoots magic waves. They turn gloomy black-and-white things into lively color.

BATTER UP, BUTTERCUP!

Hold on to your hats. Buttercup is up to bat! She can circle the bases at light speed. Good luck to anyone trying to tag her out! This spirited sport takes any and all games seriously. Buttercup is just as tough on a field as she is on crime. Nothing stands in her way.

1

TIP
Draw Buttercup playing other sports, like hockey, skateboarding, or soccer. How would her powers come in handy?

THE NEW KID(S) IN TOWN

Hey, Pokey Oaks Kindergarten! Meet your new classmate, Mike Believe. He just wants to make a friend. But the one he dreamed up turned out to be a *real* troublemaker. So the Powerpuff Girls had to send Mike's imaginary pal straight to detention. Who will be Mike's best friend now?

TIP
Try drawing Mike a new (and better) imaginary friend.

NOT WHAT THEY SEEM

The city of Townsville. A city full of average people doing average things. The Smiths are like that. This family of four lives right next door to the Powerpuff Girls. But are they *really* as average as they seem? Smile for the camera, Smith family. Your secret's safe—for now.

FACT
Mr. Smith got so tired of his boring life that he became a super-villain! Soon, the rest of his family joined him in his quest for evil.

BLOSSOM, BUBBLES, AND BUTTERCUP AT THE BEACH

Between going to school and cleaning up crime, the Powerpuff Girls sure are busy. It's fight, fight, fight in the morning. Spelling tests in the afternoon. Then Professor Utonium's bedtime story in the evening. PHEW! But even heroes need a day off, and the sisters choose to spend it together.

TIP
The girls all have different personalities. Draw what you think each would do on vacation!

1

DREAM SCHEME, BEDTIME ROUTINE

Shh . . . Draw as quietly as you can. The sun has set. The citizens of Townsville are turning in. So put on your Powerpuff pajamas because it's time for bed. That is, if Professor Utonium can get this tireless trio to settle down first!

FACT
The Powerpuff Girls and Professor Utonium live at 107 Pokey Oaks South, Townsville, USA.

31

TIP
Feeling like there's too much to draw? Focus first on the characters and the bed. Then fill out the rest of the girls' room.

2

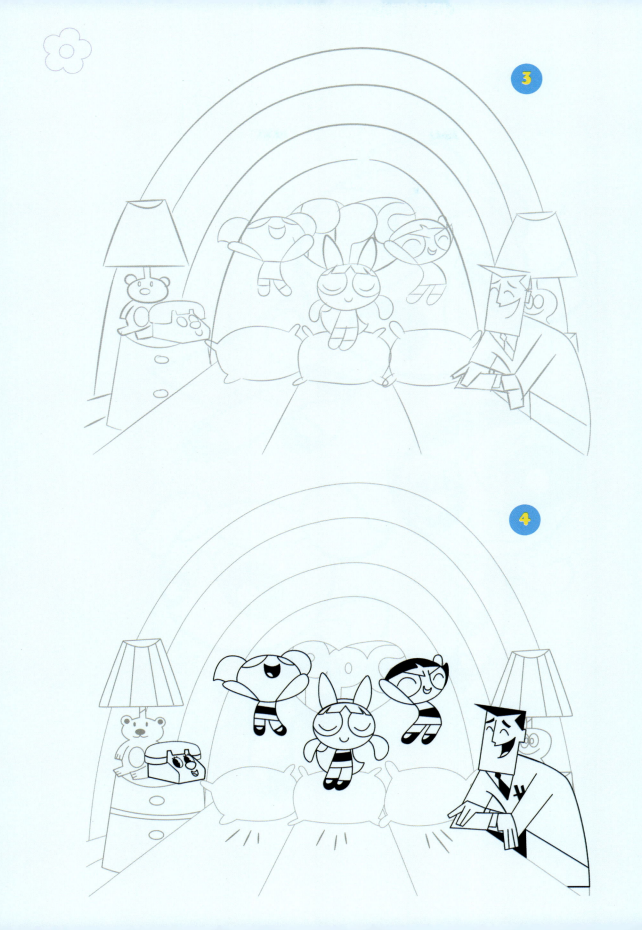

33

VILE VILLAINS

MAJOR MOJO

There once was a monkey named Jojo. He was Professor Utonium's faithful sidekick. He . . . wasn't great at it. But after an accident in the lab gave the monkey super-smarts, he changed his name to Mojo Jojo. New name, new goal! His evil mission is for apes to rule over humans. First, Townsville. Then, the world!

FACT
The Chemical X that made the Powerpuff Girls also made Mojo Jojo into the genius monkey villain he is today.

1

37

DON'T CROSS BLOSSOM!

Blossom is the leader of the Powerpuff Girls. She has a strong sense of justice and always wants to do what's right. And sometimes, the right thing is kicking some bad-guy butt! Watch out, anyone looking to do not-good. Blossom will not let you get away with it.

TIP
Blossom's bow can give your art movement. Draw it tilted when she's flying fast. Draw it straight up and down when she's standing still.

39

CASH CROWN

What Princess Morbucks wants, Princess Morbucks gets. *Almost* always. She wanted to be a Powerpuff Girl. But to do that, you've gotta be able to put the "power" in "Powerpuff"! After Princess was denied a spot as a superhero, the jealous girl turned to villainy instead. She's got big plans and a big bank account to back them up.

TIP
Princess Morbucks lives in Morbucks Manor. Draw what you think the inside looks like.

FUZZIEST FUZZY

Who's that? Oh, it's just Fuzzy Lumpkins. He's usually pretty okay—for a villain. Fuzzy spends most days napping, cooking, and making music. But when the Powerpuff Girls get on his bad side, he gets mad! So let's back away while he's in a good mood. That's it. Nobody make any sudden movements . . .

FACT
Fuzzy once joined a band made up of other Townsville villains. His favorite instrument is his banjo. Its name is Joe.

42

BUBBLES IS NO BABY

Sugar, spice, and everything nice. Those were the ingredients chosen to create the perfect little girl. Bubbles is the "sugar." She is super sweet! But that doesn't mean she's not tough too. When bad guys come out to play, she's a Powerpuff who saves the day!

TIP
Who is Bubbles fighting? The Powerpuff Girls face off against many different villains. Pick one and draw them in!

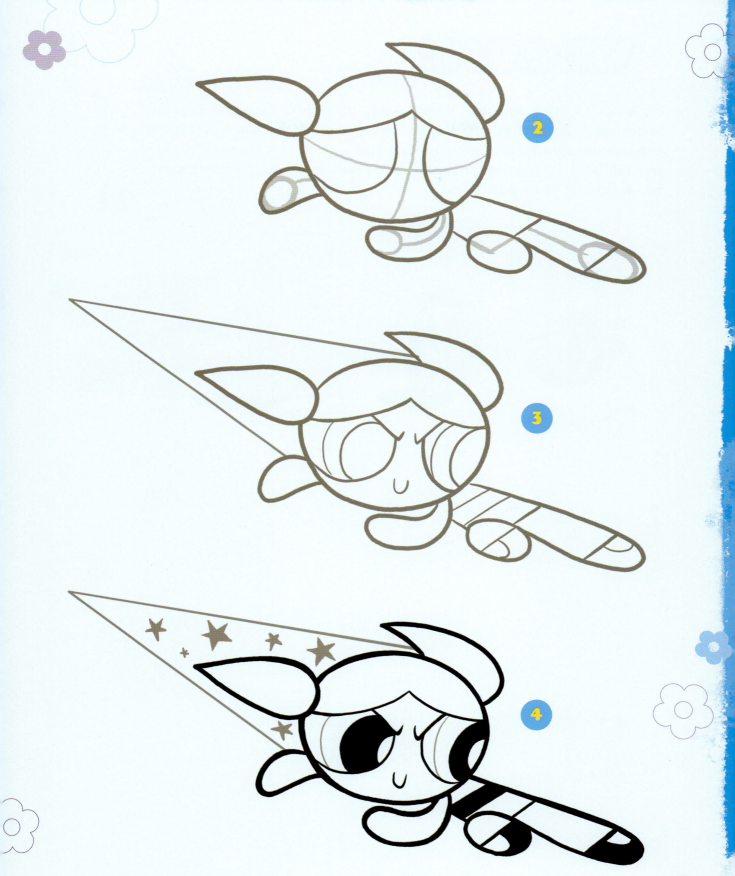

V.R.O.O.M.!

It's a K.A.R.R. It's a P.L.A.N.E. It's a T.A.N.K. It's even a R.O.B.O.T.! But most importantly, it has a built-in six-cup latte maker. With K.A.R.R., Professor Utonium thought he had built the best ride ever. It can shapeshift into any vehicle! He never imagined the smart tech would turn against him or his beloved Powerpuff Girls.

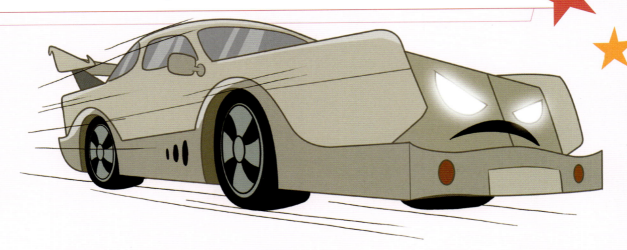

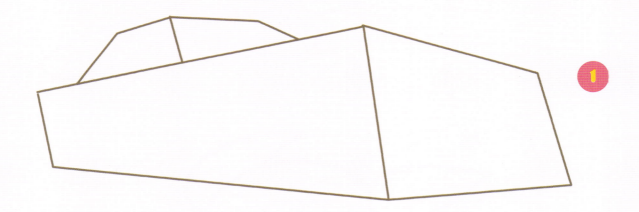

FACT
K.A.R.R. stands for Kinetic Automatic Robotic Roadster.

NOT SO FAST, MOJO JOJO

Mojo Jojo is a monkey with a plan, and he's ready to put it into action. It is a plan so evil and so diabolical that the Powerpuff Girls had better watch their step. That means they need to keep an eye on where they are putting their feet. Look out for dangerous things. Prepare for doom!

FACT
Mojo Jojo's brain is extra-large. So he wears an extra-large helmet to protect it!

48

MORBUCKS, MOREVIL

Feeling cute, might do evil later. The only thing cushier than Princess Morbucks's pigtails is her allowance—and her desire to be bad. This vain villain has got the confidence and cash to be a serious pain for Blossom, Bubbles, and Buttercup.

TIP
Princess loves buying gadgets! Draw her a jet pack, fast car, or other high-tech tool.

PERSONALITY PLUS

Fighting crime is easy. Fighting feelings is a little harder! The Powerpuff Girls may be sisters, but they have their own personalities. Bubbles is cheerful. Buttercup is brave and always ready for a fight. Blossom is confident, but even she has struggle days. (Don't we all?)

TIP
Pay attention to shapes! Small changes in the shape of the girls' eyes, mouths, and bodies can show exactly how they're feeling.

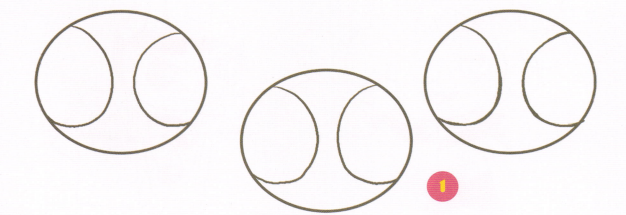

1

FEARSOMELY FUZZY

Here's a tip: Fuzzy Lumpkins doesn't like visitors, so keep off his property. Oh no. Did you get too close? I told you to stay away! Too late. He's getting mad. He's shaking with rage. And he's . . . coming this way?! Better call the Powerpuff Girls!

FACT
Fuzzy Lumpkins has a huge family. They all look a lot alike. Draw Fuzzy a new cousin!

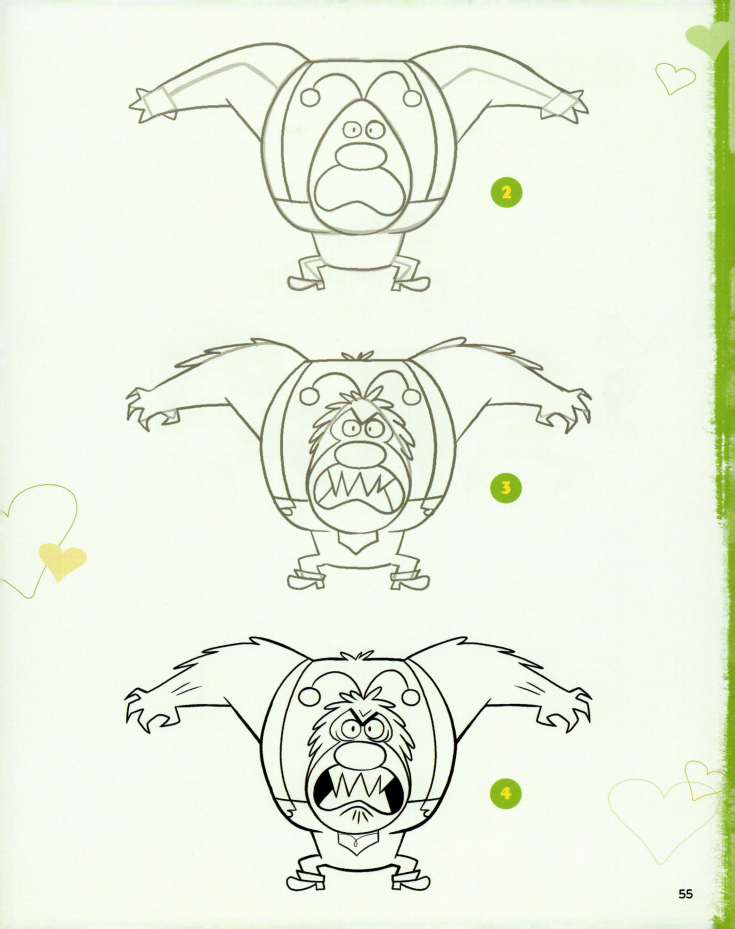

GET ROWDY

The recipe for the Powerpuff Girls is 8 cups of sugar, a pinch of spice, and 1 tablespoon of everything nice. (Plus a drop of Chemical X!) But that wasn't manly enough for Mojo Jojo. To make his own super trio, he used snips, snails, and puppy dog tails. *Voilà*! The Rowdyruff Boys were born.

TIP
Each Powerpuff Girl has a Rowdyruff Boy equal. The hairstyle details on each boy help make it clear who's who.

1

GOOD GIRLS VS. BAD BOYS

The Rowdyruff Boys thought the Powerpuff Girls would be pushovers. Think again, boys! It's Blossom, Bubbles, and Buttercup against Brick, Boomer, and Butch. Butts will be kicked and cooties will be caught in this epic three-on-three match.

FACT
Brick is the group's leader, but he's mean. Boomer loves gross stuff. And Butch never says sorry!

1

FACT
The Rowdyruff Boys have special powers. They're stronger and faster than the girls. They can make an energy blast. And they can release a cloud of toxic gas!

MEAN MONSTERS

BEWARE: BAD BREATH!

Nothing is worse than morning breath—unless you're the Toilet-Mouthed Monster! He's got a potty mouth, and he's not afraid to use it. That's very, very naughty! Will the Powerpuff Girls put him in time-out, or will he overflow and flood Townsville with foul language?

TIP
Everyone loves picking out a new toothbrush at the dentist. What style would you pick to clean up this monster's dirty mouth? Draw it in!

64

GAME ON, MONSTERS

Check it out! Buttercup is ready to kick some monster heinie. She's the toughest fighter of the sister trio. She's never afraid to jump into a brawl. It's no bluff—it's a Powerpuff! Monsters, beware. Buttercup is on her way!

FACT
Buttercup always wears lime green. It matches her eyes.

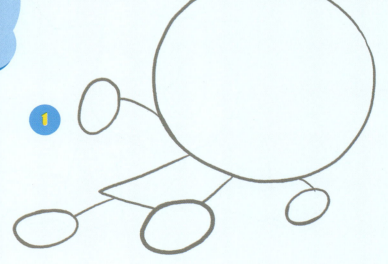

EYE SEE YOU

Look left. Look right. See anything? The Eye Monster can! It's got its eye on everyone and everything. Don't think a quick poke will stop this baddie either. Extra eyeballs on its body are ready to open up. Plus, its laser vision keeps it from getting distracted. Entering a staring contest has never been riskier!

TIP
A V-shaped eyebrow makes this brute look mad. Try turning the eyebrow upside-down. Is the monster less scary?

68

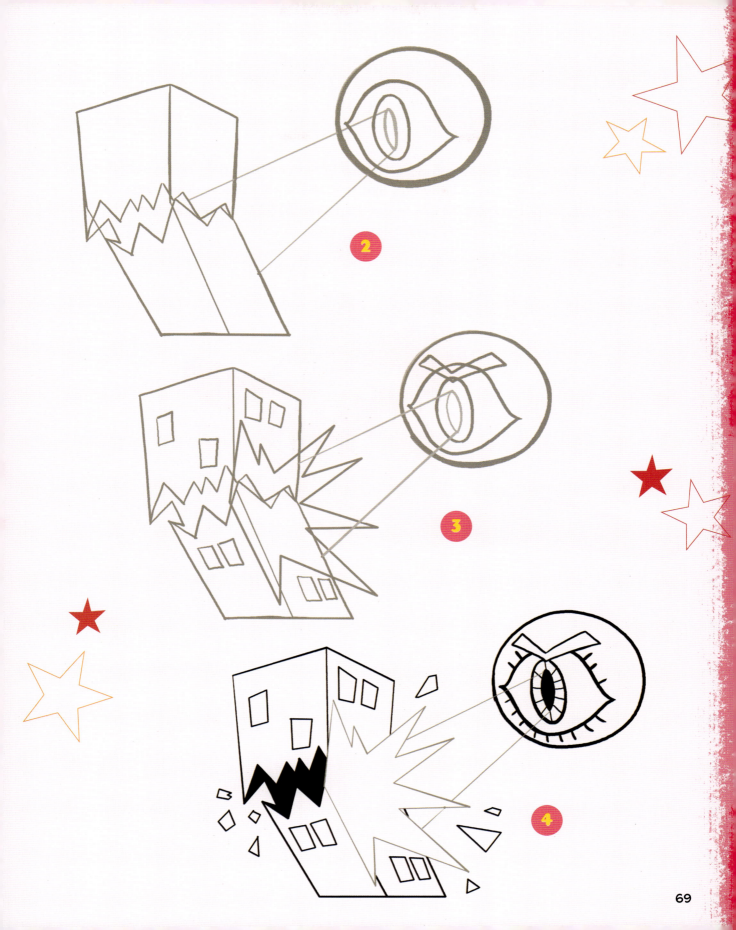

MAGGOT MONSTER MADNESS

Blossom, Bubbles, and Buttercup aren't scared of much. But they really, really, *really* don't like bugs! And a baby bug like this one is even ickier. The Maggot Monster likes to pop up in bad dreams with its evil buddy, the Boogie Man. A good squish should keep this pest away.

TIP
The Maggot Monster wears a big feathered hat. But what if it wants to switch its style? Draw a new hat. Baseball, cowboy, jester... any kind will do!

1

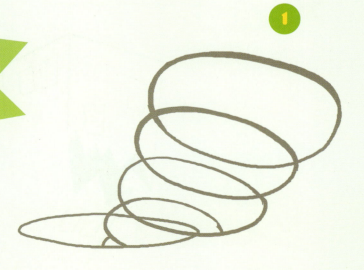

70

RSVP TO THE BIRTHDAY BOT

Every birthday party needs a giant robot, right? The villain Mojo Jojo sure thinks so. He sent the Birthday Robot to the Powerpuff Girls on their special day. The machine was wrapped up in a box with a bow. Instead of singing to celebrate, the robot went wild! It wrecked the sisters' birthday bash. Watch out for flying cake!

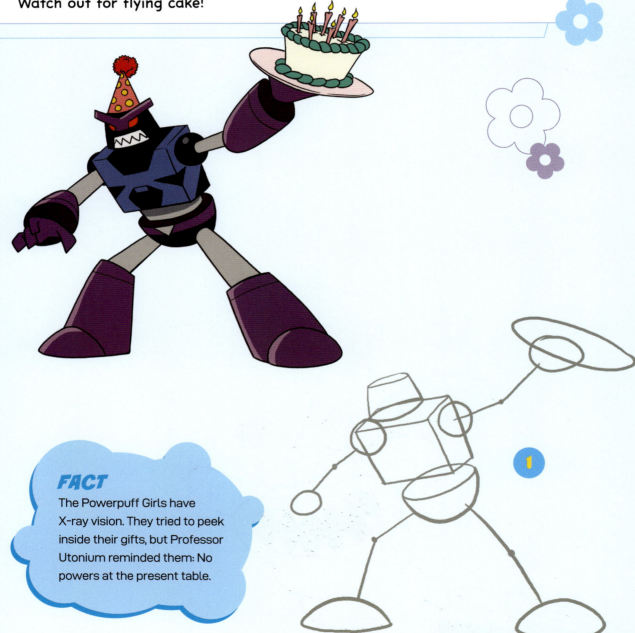

FACT
The Powerpuff Girls have X-ray vision. They tried to peek inside their gifts, but Professor Utonium reminded them: No powers at the present table.

73

CLOUDY WITH A CHANCE OF CHEESE

What's that in the sky? Is it a bird? Is it a plane? No, it's . . . alien broccoli?! The Broccoloids are here to take over the planet! The only way to fight back is by eating your veggies. Luckily, the Powerpuff Girls show the kids of Townsville how to take a bite out of crime. Pass the cheese sauce.

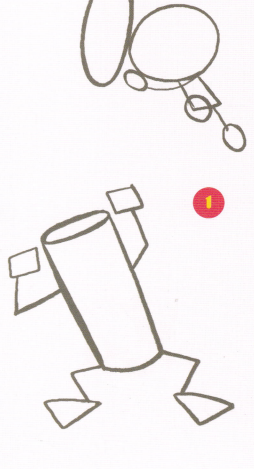

TIP

Draw the leader of the Broccoloids! He wears a belt and cape. He holds a staff with a top shaped like broccoli!

MEET THE GANGREEN GANG

Hidden deep inside the Townsville dump is a secret shack. It may be smelly. It may be dirty. But the Gangreen Gang calls it home. Ace is the group's leader. Snake is his sidekick. And Big Billy is the muscle behind the brains. A life of crime suits the gang just fine.

FACT
Big Billy is the only member of the Gangreen Gang who has red hair. His hair hides his eyes.

GANGREEN WITH ENVY

The Gangreen Gang isn't complete without Grubber and Lil' Arturo. They may be green and in the gang, but they can still be classy. Grubber doesn't only scare people for fun. He also plays the violin and speaks with a British accent! Lil' Arturo drinks coffee . . . and then gains super speed! Try keeping up with him after an espresso.

TIP
Each Gangreen Gang boy has a different hand style. Pay attention to the shapes. Those details give a character more personality.

1

BLOWUP BALLOON

Something is living in the lake. It won't nibble toes or tip over boats. But it will go on a mad rampage through Townsville! Using its huge mouth to suck in air, the Giant Fish Balloon can blow itself up to the size of a dinosaur. But like a balloon, it can be deflated just as easily. *POP!*

FACT
This big fish is covered in spikes. When the monster is full of air, its spikes shoot off in all directions.

HERE, KITTY, KITTY

Don't get between the Slime Monster and his kitty cat! The monster nearly flattened Townsville when he realized his fuzzy, fluffy *pwecious* was missing. Talk about a temper tantrum! Make sure that this never happens again. Pencil in the *purr*-fect friend every time you sketch the mound of muck.

TIP
The Slime Monster's goo is always on the move. Use wavy lines to show the dripping layers that flow down his body.

THE MONSTER MASH

The Powerpuff Girls face off against many beastly baddies. Each has its own strengths and weaknesses. Some are solid and spiky. Others are squishy and slimy. So be on guard, Blossom! Getting stuck in sludge while saving the day would be really embarrassing.

FACT
The Powerpuff Girls are girls of action! Whether it's a signature kick or fierce uppercut, they've got a finishing move ready to go.

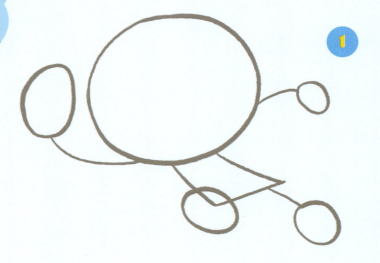

1

84

ORANGE YOU GLAD FOR ORANGES?

The Amoeba Boys want to be the masterminds behind the biggest crimes ever. Unfortunately, their brains are the size of bacteria. Bossman, Slim, and Junior's most successful heist? When they stole every orange in Townsville. People then got scurvy, like pirates of old! (Not that the Amoeba Boys planned for that to happen.) Someone call the Pow-*Arrrrrr*-puff Girls before we all have to walk the plank right to the doctor's office.

86

TIP

The Amoeba Boys don't have arms, legs, or hair. But each has a unique body shape. And their hats make it easy to tell them apart!

FACT
Townsville is home to many clever crooks... and also the Amoeba Boys. They may not be smart, but they're always up for trying a new crime!

PLAYFUL PETS

WARNING: CHANCE OF FALLING BEEBO

Professor Utonium loves to experiment. But his creations can go too far! When he tried to make the perfect pet, he ended up with BEEBO instead. This pet can only be fed once. Ever. If it gets more than one meal, it thinks of nothing but eating! It eats and eats and eats until it explodes. And that just makes more BEEBOs. On today's menu? All of Townsville!

FACT
BEEBO stands for Biogenetically Engineered Experimental Bipedal Organism.

BUBBLES WITH BUBBLES

Bubbles doesn't spend all of her time taking down bad guys. Every once in a while, she likes to take it easy. And there's nothing more relaxing than blowing bubbles. Or, maybe drawing Bubbles blowing big bubbles is even better? How many times can I say "bubbles"? Bubbles. Bubbles. *Bubbles-bubbles-bubbles*.

TIP
Make your bubbles shine! Add lines inside the circle with the same curve to show shadows and bright spots.

94

RUFF CROWD

Have you ever wondered what your dog would say if it could talk? Wonder all you want. But you might not like the answer! Talking Dog shows up around Townsville to give everyone a piece of his mind. He warns the Powerpuff Girls to watch out for the Rowdyruff Boys. He gives news interviews. This pup doesn't need anyone to tell him he's a good boy. He can do it himself!

TIP
What would your Talking Dog say? Add speech bubbles with your favorite words or phrases.

1

96

NUTS FOR BULLET

Who's the best super squirrel in the whole wide world? Bullet! She was born to a normal squirrel family. But a snack of Chemical X gave this fluffster superpowers. Fighting off a nasty hawk is no sweat. Not even the evil Mojo Jojo stands a chance against her. The woodland town of Nutsville has its own tiny protector.

FACT
Bullet loves acorns! They're a perfect snack and crime-fighting tool.

98

PRETTY WITTY KITTY

White Kitty looks sweet. That adorable tail. Those whiskery whiskers. But underneath the big ball of fluff is a soul of evil! White Kitty can hypnotize anyone foolish enough to look into his eyes. If this feisty feline had his way, cats would rule and humans would drool—after getting out the catnip, of course.

TIP
White Kitty's pupils are narrow when he's about to do evil. If he's being cute instead, make the eyes big and round.

100

PLUSHIE POWER

Octi may be a stuffed animal. But to Bubbles, he is as real as a pet can be. This four-legged friend is always there to listen, especially when the Powerpuff Girls are in the middle of a fight. Nothing brings Blossom, Bubbles, and Buttercup together like snuggling their sweet stuffie.

FACT
Octi only has four legs. A real octopus has eight!

1

102

HAPPY VALENTINO'S DAY

Did you know the Powerpuff Girls' teacher, Miss Keane, once dated Professor Utonium? The only thing that could come between the two lovebirds was the teacher's precious pet, Valentino. The Professor is no fan of felines, and Miss Keane wasn't a fan of that attitude! Better luck next time.

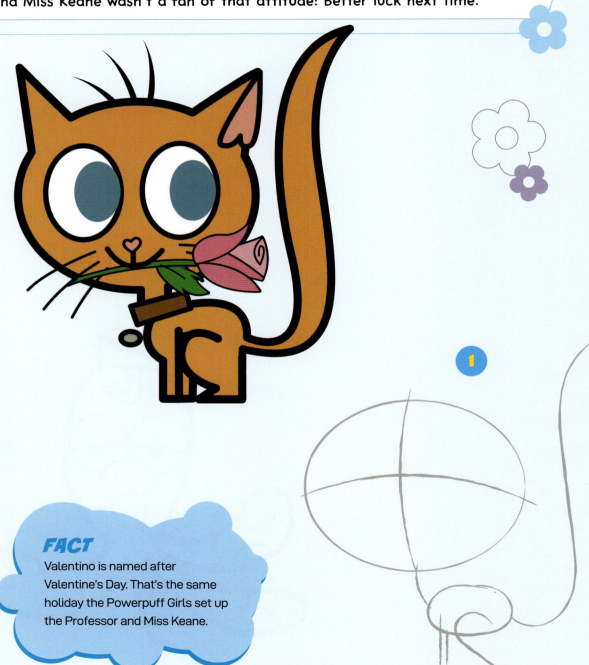

FACT
Valentino is named after Valentine's Day. That's the same holiday the Powerpuff Girls set up the Professor and Miss Keane.

BIG BABY

Bubbles loves animals so much that she cannot stop bringing them home. Other kids might show up with a dog or cat. The Powerpuff brought a baby whale! Professor Utonium doesn't allow pets in the house, but Bubbles really, really, really wants to take care of her new friend. Nobody will notice a whale playing hide-and-seek in the backyard, right?

1

TIP
What other games could the whale play with Bubbles? Draw their next activity!

FIRST OF THE FLUFF

How cute. A kitten, puppy, and bunny have joined up to make the Fluffy Bunch. Wait. What's this? Someone call the Powerpuff Girls. The Fluffy Bunch are causing trouble! Cute, cute trouble. Don't fall for those big eyes, Blossom! Oh, but that purr... Who's the fluffiest, *wuffiest*? You are, Fluffy Kitty!

FACT
The Fluffy Bunch may be fuzzy, but they do not like being cuddled. Especially not by sticky, smelly kindergartners!

109

THE PUPPY WUPPY

Make no bones about it. Puppy Wuppy is a *crook-y wooky*. This Fluffy Bunch member is always promising to be a good boy. But it's *soooo* hard. Being evil is much more fun! His best friend is Fluffy Kitty. Although neither of them wants to admit it, a cat and dog are perfect partners in crime.

1

TIP
Puppy Wuppy loves dog treats. Make him a special decorated one.

HOP TO THE SCENE OF THE CRIME

No one would suspect a bunny could lead a life of lawbreaking. But turn your back, and Cuddly Bunny will dash to do evil with her Fluffy Bunch pals. Rob a bank? Steal priceless jewels? Bankrupt Townsville? This critter is behind it all. Like all bunnies, though, there's one way to win her over—a yummy salad!

TIP
Cuddly Bunny's eyes aren't outlined in black all the way around. This makes her eyes look soft and sweet.

1

113

THE POWERPUP GIRLS

Sugar, spice, and everything nice are the main ingredients in the recipe for the Powerpuff Girls. But what kind of spices would you add for Power*pups*?! Blossom, Bubbles, and Buttercup have been turned into four-legged superheroes! Not all heroes wear capes. Some wear collars and need to go on a walk before bedtime.

FACT
Each dog's ears match the Powerpuff Girl's hair. Blossom's dog has tall ears like her bow. Canine Buttercup has small, pointy ears. The Bubbles pup has cute ears that look like pigtails.

TIP
What would Professor Utonium look like as a dog? Try drawing a Pup-fessor!

2

ABOUT THE AUTHOR

Mari Bolte is an author and editor of children's books. Whether it's a book on video games, animals, history, science, monsters, or crafts, she's always up for learning new things. (And hoping readers learn something too!) Mari lives in Minnesota with her family and far too many pets.

ABOUT THE ILLUSTRATORS

Melissa Ballesteros is an illustrator from Guadalajara, Mexico. She is best known for her work in the animation industry. Her background in film studios is shown through her use of vibrant color palettes and energetic characters, a style that also perfectly lends itself to the world of children's book publishing.

Patricio Oliver is an illustrator and a graphic designer. A graduate of the University of Buenos Aires, he has worked on books and comics as both an illustrator and writer, focusing on superhero, gender, and diversity themes. He is also a professor of typography and an assistant professor of editorial illustration, and teaches seminars and workshops for various programs.

Published by Capstone Press, an imprint of Capstone.
1710 Roe Crest Drive, North Mankato, Minnesota 56003
capstonepub.com

Copyright © 2025 Cartoon Network.
THE POWERPUFF GIRLS and all related characters and
elements © & ™ Cartoon Network. WB SHIELD: © & ™ WBEI (s25)

All rights reserved. No part of this publication may be reproduced in
whole or in part, or stored in a retrieval system, or transmitted in any
form or by any means, electronic, mechanical, photocopying, recording,
or otherwise, without written permission of the publisher.

Cataloging-in-Publication Data is available on the Library of Congress website.

ISBN: 9798875237126 (paperback)
ISBN: 9798875237133 (ebook PDF)

Summary: Go on a drawing adventure with the Powerpuff Girls!
Young artists of all abilities will have fun as they learn how to draw
the friends and foes of Townsville alongside Blossom, Bubbles,
and Buttercup through easy step-by-step instructions.

Editorial Credits
Editor: Abby Huff; Designer: Hilary Wacholz; Production Specialist: Tori Abraham

Any additional websites and resources referenced in this book are not maintained,
authorized, or sponsored by Capstone. All product and company names are
trademarks™ or registered® trademarks of their respective holders.

The publisher and the author shall not be liable for any damages allegedly
arising from the information in this book, and they specifically disclaim any
liability from the use or application of any of the contents of this book.

Printed and bound in China. 6274